Sean O'Brien

Europa

PICADOR

First published 2018 by Picador
an imprint of Pan Macmillan
20 New Wharf Road, London N1 9RR
Associated companies throughout the world
www.panmacmillan.com

ISBN 978-1-5098-4040-3

1 3 5 7 9 8 6 4 2

A CIP catalogue record for this book is available from the British Library.

Printed and bound by CPI Group (UK) Ltd, Croydon, CR0 4YY

Once Again Assembled Here was published in 2016.
He is a critic, editor, translator, playwright and
broadcaster, Professor of Creative Writing at
Newcastle University, and a Fellow of
the Royal Society of Literature.

ALSO BY SEAN O'BRIEN

Poetry

The Indoor Park   The Frighteners
HMS Glasshouse   Ghost Train   Downriver
Cousin Coat: Selected Poems, 1976–2001
Dante's Inferno: A Verse Translation
The Drowned Book   November   Collected Poems
The Beautiful Librarians   The River Road

Essays

The Deregulated Muse
Journeys to the Interior: Ideas of England in Contemporary Poetry

Anthologies

The Firebox: Poetry in Britain and Ireland after 1945 *(editor)*
Train Songs: Poetry of the Railway *(co-editor)*

Plays

Aristophanes' The Birds: A Verse Version
Keepers of the Flame   Laughter When We're Dead

Fiction

The Silence Room *(short stories)*
Afterlife *(novel)*
Once Again Assembled Here *(novel)*
The Railwayman *(graphic novel, with
Birtley Aris and Gerry Wardle)*

To Alan Brownjohn

Acknowledgements

BBC Radio 3, BBC Radio 4, *English*, *Five Poems* (Clutag Press),
Hwaet!, *New Boots and Pantisocracies*, *The Next Review*,
New Yorker, *On Shakespeare's Sonnets* (Bloomsbury), *Ploughshares*,
Poettrio, *Poetry* (Chicago), *Poetry London*, *Poetry Salzburg Review*,
Stand, *The Literary Review*, *Times Literary Supplement*, *Wild Court*.

Contents

You Are Now Entering Europa 1

Dead Ground 2

Zorn 5

The Chase 6

Away You Go 9

Apollyon 10

Signs and Wonders 12

In the Event 14

Exile 15

Goddess 16

One Way or Another 18

Madness 20

Three Views of a Secret 21

Hence, Loathèd Melancholy 23

Translation 25

Julia 27

Anniversary 28

Completists 29

Your Man 30

Wrong Number 31

The Sixties 36

The Helsinki Directive 38

Mecklenburgh Square 39

Save the Last Dance for Me 42

Terra Nostra 44

Friday the Thirteenth 46

World's End 47

Jaguar 48

Sabbatical 50

Hotel Marine 52

Hotel Voivode 54

From the Cherry Hills 56

The Sunken Lane 58

Link Boy 60

Storm Beach 62

The Calm 64

Melancholia 65

A Closed Book 68

Europa

You Are Now Entering Europa

The grass moves on the mass graves.
How many divisions has the grass
At this discreet perpetual exercise?

The fallen leaves are frozen now,
The windfalls bitter. No one writes
And I forget. I mark the days.

The grass moves on the mass graves.
I tell myself I have my work
When what I have is paper and a clock.

The grass is in the street, the street
Is at the door. I may not be disturbed,
You understand, I have my work,

So near to its conclusion now
That I will never finish it. The grass
Is at the door, is on the stairs,

Is in the room, my mouth, is me,
While I mark off the days and think
How blest I am, to have my work,

To tend the graveyard I become.

Dead Ground

In these hidden fields of heart's desire
The sheep are a rare historical breed
Who wait like royalty in exile,

Dim and fearful, crowding to the fence
For counting. There's an orchard
Drowned in waist-high grass,

That no one visits, where the apples
Make their red appeal but fall
On one another, meant

For painting, not for eating.
Down these unadopted roads
You trespass in imaginary country

Where secretly the money lives,
The Lord's anointed. Down this street
Came Hampden's men, defeated

In a hedgerow skirmish –
Old, unhappy, far-off things
Domesticated here

As *fictions to be real in.*
How did it come to be
So thoroughly possessed, this land,

This corner of a long-gone yard,
This tumbled wall of flints
That will be built again, but taller

And as though deep time
Itself might be acquired?
Likewise the hidden pool

In there among the girlish birches,
A silver blink that now you see
And now you don't,

That opens to the dreaming eye
A place within a place, a mirrored room
Where things are otherwise,

Except that in your case it won't.
See here, the forking
Of this path among the hawthorns

At the loamy patch where fungus
Levers up its cock too perfectly
Between the frosty leaves. It must be art,

The never-was and never-will,
Where ownership is all there is.
You are yourself possessed,

Except you call it geography –
And all that you have ever known,
These shut-down shires,

The liberties you think you claim
By searching out the detail
In the detail, and the nowhere

Of your six-foot plot
Itself, ends here,
This clearing in the greenwood

Where the devil sits
Enthroned on smoking ash
To count the takings.

Zorn

Somewhere in the house, I howl.
Of this much I am certain, though
These days I no longer hear.
It's only me again. Meanwhile
I watch and do not watch
The evening freight trains pull away
In almost perfect silence, gliding
At the low, inexorable speed
It's tempting if not yet compulsory
To think is that of history,
A word we'd long supposed
Was exiled to the snowfield of itself,
When all the time the patient trains
Were overhauling us to fill
This yard as big as Luxembourg,
Locked down in night and fog.
But what do I know? Only that
They roll into the tunnel, after which
No further reference is made.
There is a pause. It's me again,
There in the attic, the cellar,
Sealed between the walls, a howling
Absence of the sort you often find
In older houses such as this.
If I were me I shouldn't dwell on it
But learn to count my blessings,
Carefully and often, just in case.

The Chase

Hell might have a Function Room like this,
Where gravy fights it out with Harpic:
A mock-Tudor Midland roadhouse,
Thirties-built to meet the passing trade
Long since diverted down the bypass,
It fell on hard times, then on harder ones
And kept on falling through false floors,
Down shafts of optimistic Anaglypta,
Past the cheap and cheerful weddings,
Underbooked conventions, lingerie events
And charismatic preachers braving out
The years God turned his face away.

The old place stands in hawthorn scrub
Beside the nibbled Chase, its car-park
Dogged by doggers. It must long for arson.
What it gets are damaged veterans
And others of uncertain provenance,
Would-be *Werwolfs*, left behind
To serve the cause from bunkers dug
Beneath allotments their St George's flags
Announce are Ingerland no more.
There will be those who speak, who bring
Fraternal greetings from 'our Flemish friends'
And those who listen with a hope so long
Deferred it is immortal. What began
One pale late summer evening here

Will end when darkness brings instructions
To prepare for the eternal Soon,
The ur-time worshipped in the true
Theology where things are otherwise.
But in the meantime minutes must be taken,
Grist to the banal resentments,
Nudges, localized atrocities, as omens of
The greater cause, and let no one forget
That there are windows to be licked
And public discourse to be joined
Until, on average eighteen seconds in,
The call's cut off at Radio Chase ('It's where
The middle of the Midlands is') again.

These are the relatives you never see now
Since your parents' generation died.
You do remember, yes, the awkwardness —
A funeral tea held somewhere like the Chase,
That might have even been the Chase,
A flyblown nowhere, birches, ponds,
With HGVs parked up in laybys full of rubbish
And a sense that give or take this could be
Any time since 1931.
And someone's husband joining you outside
To smoke, assuming you'd agree
With his shy-smiling bigotry about
'Our friends from the subcontinent.'
You can't remember what you said. You can,
And it was nothing, while he stood his ground
There in the carpark, and if he sensed

That you were clenching with embarrassment
You couldn't tell. He'd made his point,
While you declared you'd better make a start
And he advised what roads you should avoid,
And never blinked, while here in hindsight
You're still blinking at the shame of it
When accident has brought you back
Down these unfashionable routes,
And then contrived the need to stop
And get a sandwich.
                           Sunday afternoon
In Albion's excluded middle.
The meeting is concluding on the far side
Of the corridor. The literature is all there
At the back beside the runes and ornamental
Daggers that make lovely gifts. To say it takes
All sorts may be a fallacy, but here they are
And here you are, again. The sandwich comes.
You watch them load their tat and nonsense
Back into the knacker's van. You are confused
By a persistent disbelief that this
Can be the case, this levee of Poujadists
Dawdling by their cars till those with homes
To go to go there, and those with holes
Hole up to count the days till their black sun
Rises on this honest plain of Midland
Ash and spoil and their inheritance is saved
From everyone, including you.
Too bored to laugh, too tired to cry, you think
These people do not matter. Then they do.

Away You Go

Then when you find you disagree,
And when they hang you in the street,
Remember: solidarity
Was once the ground beneath your feet,
And now you're dancing on the air
For hangmen, hangmen everywhere.

Apollyon

'I perceive thou art one of my subjects.'
Pilgrim's Progress

Evening comes. He steps out now
Through the damp green door
At the foot of the bridge

To walk abroad – for dogs,
For girls, for rickety drunks
And a Turkish waiter simply lost

In the park's dim valley –
All grist to his will.
Grind the bones, stir in the blood.

In the guise of a nineteenth-century
Gent of an antiquarian bent
He rises as though from the grave,

Still hale, sword-stick to hand.
Soon everywhere will crave
A bespoke assassin like this in black,

A chap one might take for a cleric,
A scholar, or even perhaps
For a fool, who of course is the fatal

Exception who proves the rule,
As many a one might attest,
Apollyon, as he proves to be —

For what is this place
And what are you
But a genre piece at best? —

Whose burning gaze is reason,
Who creates necessity.
There he is, see,

In the eye of the bridge —
The personage you least expect
And yet have always waited for,

Who will be strict in his arrest.

Signs and Wonders

from the Rubovian

The cranes have ceased to fly.
They dismantle themselves
Like funfair rides, and prepare now
To wait out the winter
Somewhere at the back of everything.
I mean, they're only birds.

*

There are wolves on the edge of the Town Moor,
Green-eyed in the birchwoods,
On tiptoe, just testing the market.
Better throw them a sheep. She'll do.

*

This word you keep saying: *hospital*.
What does it mean?
Because we've never heard of it.
Likewise this *common good*.
How could that be? Have you been drinking?
How will you pay your urine tax?

*

If the hangmen didn't I'm sorry
Then someone else would.
They're simply *in situ*
With all their equipment
Going to waste. It's common sense. Amen.

*

I see you, my thin blue friend.
It's no good standing sideways on –
The tail is a giveaway really –
Likewise the jar of piss
You want us all to thirst for.
We must seem such ungrateful cunts.

In the Event

An afternoon of bitter cold,
Blue for an hour, then black, with stars
Like braziers on battlements
By which we are excluded and enclosed.

Time slows. What must happen makes ready.
Time now to avert the gaze,
Attending not to great affairs,
The falling kings, the death of states,

But to the interests of the mind, the heart,
In what is called imagination. Now
Before it is forbidden
I take up my book, and now

My hands are burning,
Skin recoiling from the flesh, an agony
In which the difference between
The fire and the ice escapes me.

Exile

You had nowhere to go. Nowhere was best.
The bread is salty, as befits the portion
Handed to an exile when his novelty is gone
And letters from the capital have ceased.

Does pessimism of the intellect outbid
The optimism of the will at last?
Your only shirt is flying at half-mast
Where you have come to rest, among the sheds

And mongrels of an old allotment
No one seems to own or need to bomb.
It is from here, perhaps, that change must come.
You are garrotted by a man your hosts have sent.

Goddess

Just you and me, then, but mainly you,
In the overgrown archway of ivy and jasmine,
One hand gathering your skirt above the dewy grass,
And your crown of white roses afloat on the air
At six a.m., when my breath clouds with frost
And the burnt gold leaves of the silver birch
Are chattery and slick from last night's storm,
And always there is something I desire
But cannot name.
                    It would not be true if I said
You are walking away, since I am less present to you
Than the stones you glide over. Goodbye then.
How long has this been going on? Time and again
I wake and watch you passing by
In that invulnerable privacy, the sight of which
I used to believe was a gift you bestowed,
While inside the gift was a promise
That all should be well in the garden,
And the garden be shown as the sum of all things.

For all that other girls I've known resemble you,
Those quiet prefects placing flowers
On a speech-day stage or on a grave,
Or knowing the steps of the dances, taking hands
Or turning Fury to denounce and freeze the blood,
You are here anyway, here in the first place,
Unknowable, not to advise or console,

Seen from afar at less than arm's length, the dear
Inhuman girl-goddess you are, without rancour or pity.
I do know the rules. And yet I need
Your absolution: failing that, the power
Of your pure unseeing gaze to do
As you have done with me, and to forget.

One Way or Another

One way or another at this late stage
I must have them all back, those lost afternoons
In the hawthorn wood on the quarry floor
With the scent like musk, like Shalimar,
With the attic also, where love took place,
With the fall of your hair
When you'd marked your page,
Over the pillow and over the grass,
With the look on your face when you called my name
As if that word were entirely new
And I answered in kind
And that was enough, it was world without end.

Where did we go when the old year died?
We eluded ourselves. Where did we hide?
Landfill, riverbed, passage of time,
Somewhere whose name can never be said.
Yet I must trace the stairs again
From the attic room to the quarry floor
Though no such places exist, any more
Than the rain that fell on your sleeping face
When I covered you up
With my coat and saw
The rose-flush fading on your skin,
But not that this was a moment of grace.

What business of ours who are gone
Can it be if the past keeps faith,
If the may-tree's scent and the rain evoke
The lost look on your face when you awoke
In the evening wood, in the attic room,
As if they amount to the true address
Where secretly we're living?
I think on the whole I have nothing to say,
I am old and ill, have gone away.
What is this if not more of the same,
When the merciless ghosts insist
That if I dare listen, I'll hear my name?

Madness

Took one tab too many and you lost your place.
The last I heard, you were haunting auctioneers
For giant wardrobes you'd no room to house.
The last I heard. It must be thirty years.

Step through another giant door, push past
The overcoats that hide the streetlamp in the wood
Where it has snowed a century.
Lie down again, and close your eyes and rest.

You were never really going out with me.
I cannot save you. I never could.
Blue dusk. Snow falls. You must be cold. You won't be told,
My crone, my beauty, ruined child.

Three Views of a Secret

after Sonnet 94

i

Is it that all you are is beautiful,
The world your elegant sufficiency,
A balcony on which you may arrive
Spontaneously once more to blind us all
With your neglectful gaze – *choose me, choose me* –
Itself an end, which means we are alive
To suffer in the service of the will
You do not choose to exercise? Do tell.
The stars' exertions staring down the dark
Are all extinguished by comparison
With your implacable indifference.
Show us again, *show me*, the cruel sense
You make, although I know there can be none,
Then when I sicken, kill me with a look.

ii

The mirror is expecting you. You're late.
Should silver blacken, flesh give up its bone,
Time will attend you still, and after that
More time, when all your suitors go to dust.

It is a law and strikes down both the just
And the unjust, pronouncing them the same
Poor tenants of your comfortless estate.
Oh all the rest are gone like a rehearsal.
The mirror waits for you to come to pass.
To think they said you could not have it all:
As you have learned from gazing in the glass,
The mirror waits. It waits for you alone.
The only answer to this world is one.

iii

When you consume yourself away, the room
Grows sober in the aftermath. The light
Falls plainly on the bare bed and the chair.
Now it might seem that you were never there.
Your exit, like your law, is absolute,
Your legacy intolerable calm,
The blaze of noon identical with night
And ecstasy the servant of despair.
You will not serve the downcast god of love:
That great refusal is a gift I crave.
Yours is the power to steal the world away
And to possess what might have been its soul
In patience, as one might possess a grave
Before the spade has even pierced the soil.

Hence, Loathèd Melancholy

Tonight I will wear my new waistcoat
To the party. You will wear your cloak.
We will put on masks and be amused
By friends we fail to recognize.
This will all be a lie, told in good humour
For the best of reasons. I will dance
With his squeeze, and he with you
In a temporary climate known as
Mutually supportive fraudulence,
To compensate for recent disappointment
And the eerie loss of texture that suggests
A dimension sold off on the quiet.
Harlequins and Columbines
Will take the floor and recombine
And while the music lasts, its spell
Will stop us noticing the smell.

Hence, loathèd Melancholy. Let's be
Barefaced. We've practised and we try
To make the best of things, and it's a lie,
And everybody's at it anyway.
Hier nicht, nicht hier. Hier nicht, nicht hier.
Yes, there have to be economies.
Everything drains from the pocket –
Pence, pus, principle, as fish rots
From the head, and as the Secretary of State
Sings 'Swastika Eyes' in the bath.

If we elect to *drink and dance and screw*
The lie is as plain as your face and yet
Quite incomprehensible. Drink this
And kiss me, darling. Lie with your
Long tongue, with your nyloned legs.
Lie to the music, to the air itself,
And lie beside me later, silent. Lie.

So maybe long ago I would admit
No separation of realms between
The people with the guns and money
And your choice of rosy lipstick,
But everyone knows better now the lie
Has grown into its birthright and is free
To share its meretricious bonhomie
In a Borgia's poisoned handshake.
At the end of the evening the lie goes home
As a growth on the back of the head
We mistake for ourselves. It needs no sleep,
Lying there telling itself in the dark,
And in the steamy compact mirror
Madame Secretary addresses in the bath
While whispering 'Swastika Eyes'
At dead of night, because she can, a song –
Hier nicht, nicht hier. Hier nicht, nicht hier –
Which (this part's true) she knows by heart.

Translation

after AEH

No, we were never introduced,
Yet she and I were long acquainted.
I know all her ways and all
The tunes this pale usurper sings
To those she has seduced
Beneath the blanching mays
And left, like her, demented.
So eminently natural
That even nature must defer
Before her instinct to conserve,
In leopard shoes and silver rings
The maenad roves out now
To see into the life of things
And sow her poison at the root,
To claim the earth, to claim the air,
To rid the world of witnesses
Until, in her divine enclosure,
She alone is there.
No, we were never introduced.
What purpose could I serve?
I am no one she'd remember,
Being the merest subject, left –
Far more than I deserve –
To wander in her private grove

Until her work was done.
Now, in the aftermath of love,
The world is all December:
This is trespass: I must go,
And may the heartless, witless
Creature neither care nor know.

Julia

It is not to be understood
That we walk the dogs you never met
In a Christmas gale on the freezing shore
Below the shuttered Rendezvous Café,
Nor that you cannot be found there making notes
While possessed of an overwhelming need
To be in several other places too.
This grey day the lights at St Mary's and Tynemouth
Stand unblinking, and the tide
Goes out impossibly far too far
Ever to come in. And meanwhile
You have left the building –
The Rendezvous, Percy, Live, the RVI –
And a hush of disappointed electricity
Waiting for the circuit to be opened
Once again. *But that's all right,*
You are insisting somewhere else
As you race through your stowed-out diary,
The dreadful miracle's all right –
Though do beware of makey-uppy stuff.
Such as? Such as that on a stormy day
I see you climb to the mad crow's nest
On the roof of the Armstrong Building
And place one hand on the iron rail
And the other on the conducting rod.
Oh, lightning can strike twice, you say. *Watch this.*

Anniversary

Now you've been dying as long as you lived.
The hoarfrost's back on the railway path.
The allotment bincinerator's doffing and doffing
Sombreros of smoke. C'est superbe. Magnifique.

But this is not life, not the whisky and the acid
And the speed and the snuff and the other stuff
Laid out ceremonially, like you with the coins
On your eyes, with the child support and the taxman owed

And the wives – so many they form a procession,
Girls of the sixties, done up to the nines
In black nylons and chiffon, with floppy black hats,
Compliant in the fantasy as used to be

Their inclination, pausing only long enough
For each to cast a black rose down the pit behind you
Plain as day, as tangible as gin and lipstick. Gone.
This is the shortest day. The hoarfrost crackles

And the bin has smoked itself almost to death.
Now a metro glides past, an empty one, bound
For the depot. You liked a big finish, my friend.
Now you've been dying as long as you lived.

Completists

for R.L.

Somebody has to remember the OK band
With five good songs and two LPs.
By accident we saw them live one night
On a 'short autumn tour' of seaside toilets.
Somebody had to, and that would be us.

They were outside afterwards smoking a joint
In the lee of the van. We approached for a word.
The balding lead guitarist didn't want to share
And the drummer delivered a harrowing talk
On the high cost of touring. He's dead now.

They were good, though, good for thirty people,
For opening with new material we sensed
Would never be recorded. We know their name,
How they never sold out, how the walls of the dump
Fell away, and for an hour it was beyond dispute
That art is all there is and might not be enough.

Your Man

Your man is waiting on the landing now.
Black overcoat buttoned to keep in the cold,
He nods as if admitting you this once.

You've read the book and here he is,
Extremely so, the patient creditor, on hand
To repossess the place in its entirety –

Fixtures, fittings, decorations,
Sitting tenants and the memories
They claim are theirs. It's down in writing.

Oh, he is all the time in the world,
But now and then he glances at the watch
He never wears. Or you may catch him

Turning to a page with nothing on it,
Or sometimes, in the deepest afternoon,
Asleep, it seems, the mucus ticking in his throat.

Wrong Number

HD, KS, JHW

i

Nobody there but white noise and old weather,
The faint breath of time ticking over.
I ought to hang up, but there follows

The second-hand sound of an ancient tram
Arthritically cornering, close to the Wall,
A part we never visited but I appear to know

As if I lived there. One more friend is gone.
There goes the tram I heard but never saw
And with it comes the view from nowhere,

From those tall, prohibited depositories
In grey, shell-pocked Wilhelmine stone,
Where air and dust were placed under arrest

Until such time as Fascism was dead
And all the apparatus of the state
Could lock itself away and be forgotten.

ii

In April in a heatwave when we passed
Through Checkpoint Charlie we became
No more ourselves than the green-faced Vopos

Glaring from their booths, afraid to sweat.
We stood there in the centre of the world,
The street where it would end, the omphalos

Of realpolitik. I had nothing in mind
But that I was unequal to the challenge
No one issued as we blundered affably along

Past blown-off cornerstones and gates
To courtyards that you would not lightly enter.
We found a café where the silence paused

Politely while we ate the gluey torte.
The waitress hid. The furniture inspected us
In case we might bring trouble to the door.

We were sensible, modest and spoke
In low voices, said nothing and at last
Arrived on the Museum Island

Where the sooty dome was foundering
Beside the Spree. The Pergamon was shut.
But this was culture. It was culture

That disposed of Rosa Luxemburg
In the canal, a little to the south? the west?
Where we would not be going anyway.

The heat was filthy. On the balconies
Of workers' flats the flags hung limp
As Mayday neared, the last, though we

Could not have told. I tried and failed
To hand my Ostmarks back as we returned,
Then found a toyshop off the Ku'Damm

Where I bought a mouse in shirt and trousers
For the daughter of a friend – from hundreds
Dangling from the ceiling by their necks

Like miniatures from Plötzensee,
Where men were hanged on hooks with wire
And filmed by other men for the amusement

Of their masters. I chose not to mention this
Because it was too obvious or literary,
Like making something out of nothing

For the sake of poetry, as if that were a sin.
I had nothing to add, I would later read,
'But a species of moral exhaustion'.

[33]

iii

We got no story in the East beyond the wide
Depopulated streets, with trams we heard
Yet never glimpsed. The walk we took

Was simply one more form of waiting.
Agents, patients, we were neither, merely there
In transit for an hour or two and scarcely

Worth recording, but the telephone
Proves faithful to the death. Once more
It clears its throat of static. Message ends.

I lie awake like a receiver. No one called
Or talked about 'the old days' in Berlin
Where nothing happened but the weather and the smell.

The group was never in one room again
And you and you and you are dead
Although you were supposed to live for ever.

Time breathes its last repeatedly: the tram
Is still a block away. No message, no reply.
When I went back, the GDR was over

And the bookshop where I read had opened
On the ground floor of a warehouse
By the Wall. I was impressed, until the manager

Confided that the place was doomed already:
IG Farben's agents were in court to seek
The restitution of the larger property,

A breathless cave of dust, the status quo.
It might be irony, though who can tell
If history enjoys such flourishes

Or else has disappeared itself as easily
As someone ushered down a corridor,
Like you and you and you? And either way

How does a silent call at 4 a.m. connect
With anything? I hear the tram approach
The corner where the bricked-up windows

Are not meant to look, my friends –
No matter where it goes nor who's aboard
Or to what purpose, with what outcome.

I'm still here. I answer and attend
To no one and to nothing, yet as though
The silence is a proof or a rebuttal.

The Sixties

It's five o'clock. The world is happening.
The faces of the flatmates pass across the glass

As they prepare for life. This evening might be
Serious, they can't tell yet. From other flats

Comes other music or the silence of the old.
This is perfection, the great not-yet, the mystique

They will learn to distrust, but the cab's in the street.
There's a clatter of heels on the stairs, and now

The room and the river of cabs below, the bright eyes
And the lipstick have all done their work.

*

Shall she outlive the names of the clubs
And the odd little place they discovered

With nobody there but themselves – the one
Where the afternoon cut off the phone?

Will she manage it, tangible as gin and lipstick
And a morsel of mascara in the corner of one eye?

Is she permitted, can she afford, to be particular,
Waiting in the mirrored lift that smells of smoke

While it descends, descends and utters her
In Gower Street at dusk, to frost in the air

And the fumes of exhaust ascending in cowls,
Or are she and her gladrags history too?

The pub on the corner knows, and the barman
Who turns as she enters, as if this was not on the cards,

And is quiet and tactful, unbearable nearly,
Like death when he's showing a lady his good side,

While she assembles her resources on the counter-top
And knows she has begun to wait. All done.

The Helsinki Directive

In the movie I'll discover you, Professor,
In your dim conservatory, naked
But for a towel, your spectacles steamed up
And in your ear an ice-pick.
I dare say you'll recognize this
As I will recognize my journey here
Across the frozen lake beyond the playground
Where the giant apparatus stands
Like crucifixes or the wheels employed
For breaking heretics. No one will be there,
The snow will be falling again
And you will have nothing to add.
The mysterious beauty in the champagne mink
Will be somewhere in the offing –
In the sauna, perhaps. I dare to hope.
She will have kept her hat on, naturally,
And under it a weapon. Though the Cold War
Hinges on this dark encounter, I
See me thinking mainly with my dick
And to an infinitesimal degree about
The fact that only in aesthetic terms
Can I be justified. No road but this,
To plunge beneath the ice with her.
Years later, as I too am done away with
I will see this little episode as what
Makes me immortal, skating
Gingerly across the snowy lake, aroused
By sex stroke death, and still not there.

Mecklenburgh Square

I roamed the streets of London town,
Afflicted with the blues,
For I was blocked like a Chelsea drain
And forsaken by my Muse.

The plates on every door I passed
Announced: *Psychiatrists*.
Now I may be sick, I may be mad,
But I'd sooner slash my wrists

Than blow my wad on Freud and Jung
For want of company,
But an outdoors girl who knew the ropes
Might do the trick for me –

And I met a young lady in Mecklenburgh Square,
A beautiful shrink with long black hair.
I said, 'So what do you fancy, Miss?'
A barley wine
Will do you fine,
And after that a kiss.

'Do not presume,' the lady said,
'To know what I desire.
I am autonomous and it may not
Be you that I require.

'But since you're offering I'll take
A dot of ruby port
And you can try to prove to me
That you're a decent sort.'

'Now that I would not claim,' I said.
'I'm a poet to the core.'
'Is that a fact?' She shook her head.
'Come close and tell me more.'

I laid out all my troubles then
And she was all concern.
On such a night what can you do
But let the money burn?

A barley wine will do you fine,
And after that a kiss.
A dot of red will turn your head
And then it goes like this:

The Lamb, the Sun, the Moon, the Stars
And all them other places —
We took in all the four-ale bars
Till we were off our faces.

'What kind of shrink are you?' I said,
'Who goes out on the lash?'
'A thirsty one,' herself replied,
'And now I have to dash.'

She vanished like euphoria
And I never got that kiss.
So watch out, lads – the likes of her
Will only take the piss.

I walked my empty pockets home
And swore I'd quit the booze,
For a Mecklenburgh psychiatrist's
A damned expensive muse,

And yet I find I tend to wander
Back through Mecklenburgh a while,
For though she took me for a mug
She had a certain style.

The Lamb, the Sun, the Moon, the Stars
And all them other places –
We took in all the four-ale bars
Till we were off our faces.

A barley wine will do you fine,
And after that a kiss.
A dot of red will turn your head.
The old song goes like this.

Save the Last Dance for Me

For D.H.

Masquers, slowly dancing, torchlit, on the furthest quay.
Arlecchino, Colombina, Puncinello, Il Dottore.

The fever in the blood has thickened to an ooze
But still – see there – it burns, about the eyes and fingertips

And when the lady turns away and back and licks her lips.
The ultimate infirmity is needing not to choose.

*

There are sins of the flesh. There are lies of the mind.
Each betrayal is paid in kind.

Il Capitano, La Signora, Scaramouche.
First with the daughter, then with the wife,

With the blue-black kiss of a fisherman's knife.
Tincture of mercury. Scald and douche.

Time they were gone. Too soon for dawn.
Gates of ivory? Gates of horn.

*

Unlisted it would seem in *la Commedia dell'Arte*,
You, sir, what do you bring to the party?

Crossing the marsh in your weightless craft,
With a gaze that glitters like burning gold,

In a hand as ancient as the oar you hold
You have already finished the final draft.

Terra Nostra

One of the desert states. A road
Where all day nothing passes.
Altocirrus. Blue. The vast
Prison built by emptiness
Makes Fascists of them all.
In decommissioned silos half-
Forgotten by the military,
The Aryan Brotherhood perfects
A form of crystal meth
That was already perfect,
Sky-stealers sampling the blue
For the blue it has yet to confess.
Why should they not have their visions?
Who's to stop them, motherfucker?
The function of the slide guitar:
To manufacture authenticity
From stony roots and succulents
And claim the air of imminence
That is the only thing that makes it
Bearable to watch the serpents
And the lizards labour to transcend
The asinine magnificence
Of mere geography. Downstairs
Only Metal is admitted
To the sanctum where the hedonists
Make laws from mere indulgence,
With shots of messed-up Emo chicks

Pinned to the wall like souvenirs
From other worlds and higher sentiments.
Sooner or later these bad boys
Will feel the call to break on through
And hunt each other down
In pitch-black corridors. So now
You know as much as we do, sport.

Friday the Thirteenth

Full-skirted lime-trees here, and the lilac,
That was late beginning, burnt to popcorn.
Storm coming, the authorities declare.
Better to be gone. Better to be nowhere.
When the host of the righteous attacks
You will wish you had never been born.
Now you reassure yourselves that yes,
You were the first of the prescient few
Who could tell where it leads, from a dust-devil
Spinning in a noon-hot market-place,
A detail seen from space as merely true
Among the infinitely lone and level
Sands where time begins and ends.
My infinitely clever friends,
If being right is its own reward
Your ironic composure will not save
Your skin from the wrath of the vengeful horde
Or your bones from an unmarked grave.

World's End

And anywhere at all will do
To bring it off, to see it through
From soup to nuts via the gods
And all the other odds and sods
Not needed on the voyage, so
Fire the sunset gun: let's go,
A positively final tour
Of what we know now as before –
Not to presuppose an after.
Let's make a present of our laughter
To darkness closing in behind.
If we should linger, night won't mind,
For the distinguished thing is done
As if we'd none of us begun
At all, and never travelled here
To pause before we disappear,
To make, for once, the apt remark,
Then lightly step into the dark.

Jaguar

A man with the head of a jaguar
Sits at the bar. He has read all the papers
And drunk too much coffee, and still it is early,
But now, by the patterns he plays with his hands
On the brass bar-rail, and the twin
Bass-drum pedals of his great hind paws
On the rung of the bar-stool, what he can hear
Is a different music: neither the apologies
Delivered by the barrel organs, nor the vaunts
Of the *narcocorridos*, nor yet the appeals
For vengeance in the name of love preferred
By the stations that cleaners and cab-drivers
Tune to when searching for something
Resembling silence in Mexico City. The jaguar
Purrs, he growls, and on the stroke of noon
He sips Pacifico and goes on waiting.
The waves of percussion surge and hold,
While *chicas* and matrons, the bankers, the beggars,
The cops and the military armed to the teeth,
Pass up and down the magic radii extending
From Zocalo to the furthest slum. So who
Will dare to ask the jaguar if he performs
Requests, and might be called upon to sing aloud
The song that ripples through the fur
And muscle his white shirt and sober charcoal suit
Cannot disguise, the song of death and paradise?
Will you? As if the jaguar can tell

Merely by glancing your way as you pass,
He shakes his head, just barely, and his golden stare,
Although it means you are unworthy
Even to appeal to hear that secret music,
Nonetheless agrees that all of us are born
To live in hope despite the mounting evidence.

Sabbatical

In August the Department empties.
You notice how the echoes simply stop
As in a council swimming pool
Earmarked for redevelopment
Yet every year mysteriously spared
In late September, by which time
I shall be gone. I shall be gone.
Astray along the lonely corridors,
The lunatics who stick it out
In mortal terror of the REF
Profess their manias to noticeboards
And piles of broken furniture:
Civis, civitas, civility, and jam tomorrow.
But in August only rich and silent
Conscientious Chinese students come,
To witness with their grave politeness
How the West declines and does not read.
Après moi, Creative Writing, dammit.
Good luck, my friends, my enemies,
And those of you to whom in all these years
I've still not spoken. Now I bid farewell,
Abandoning my desk, my books
And thirteen thousand frantic e-mails
Enquiring about the Diary Exercise
On which the fate of everything
(To whit, this institution) hangs
And threatening to equip me for

The Challenges Ahead: *so why not let us*
Have your brain to fuck about with?
Alas, I must decline. I leave instead
My Nurofen and rehydration salts,
My postcards (Nietzsche, Audrey Hepburn)
And my locked and darkened room,
Just when, after a year of vain appeals
To Maintenance, my broken radiator
Starts to clank, as prisoners use cutlery
To speak from cell to cell by night,
As though a language I no longer know
Or love might yet detain me here,
When I and my Senior Railcard are bound
For Cythera and *luxe* and *volupté* at last.

Hotel Marine

You must watch another hour before descending,
With your page unwritten, to the heat
That's not quite finished with the day,

Then take your table in the courtyard
Where the others sit, each islanded
With last week's papers and their tablets,

The widow reading, and the German lesbians
In aviator shades, and men of sixty
Hard to place except that they resemble you.

The whisper of the sea is close enough from here.
The guests will all look up and look away
And catch the shadow slowly being drawn

Across the marbled space, the first faint stirring
In the palms, and in the dark interior
The waiter woken from suspended animation.

In the city through the arch, preserved
Like dignity that no one notices,
The shuttered bookshops wait for night

Or arson, sealed on dim, immobile air,
Their labyrinthine shelving crammed
With uncut volumes – the vanilla scent

That some call history but is neglect —
By the thousand or ten thousand poets
Who were here in rooms like yours, or later

In their indigence stretched out beneath
The baking tiles, to prove their ignominy
Worth the candle, honoured to have failed.

The roof of shadow closes and the bar's
Blue jail is once more open. Out there
Beyond the arch, the lines of palms extend,

The jetties, citadels and paired-off sphinxes,
Sea walls, flags, the Pharos on its causeway
And the final stones that punctuate the blue

Like leader-dots, the last of them
Too far out now to place with certainty
At dusk among the ferries and the water's

Fading contours, so that soon you cannot tell
If you've already made the voyage they propose,
Or if instead the sea has sailed away.

Hotel Voivode

Homage to Barry Unsworth

The dining chairs tilt forward
Like half-pay cavalry officers
Slumped in their weary red jackets,

Men short of a war, who mean
To drink themselves to death
Until, unless – no matter – the next begins.

The peace grinds pitilessly on.
Flies study the menu. I study the flies,
And the cook and the chambermaid

Study me. Thus is maintained
The balance of power, and now
I know what fifty years are made of.

Once a week as is the law
I send my threadbare digest,
Wrapped in oilcloth, wedged

Inside an olive-barrel, off
Towards the capital whose name,
Regime and geographical

Location have all altered
More than once since I began.
No news is good news, I affirm.

Whatever word's sent back
Is lost or else abstracted
By an enemy. And yet I live,

And lock away the thought that no
Reply has ever come, for then
This dim hotel, this silent street,

Would be the sum of things,
And that way madness lies.
I keep the faith. I live on air.

I'll go on watering the ink
Until it vanishes with me
Into the archives of oblivion

Where blind historians
Play scissors, paper, stone —
Because I chose perfection of the work

Or it chose me, and in return
The daughter of the chambermaid
Has changed from whore to nurse.

From the Cherry Hills

At dawn in this beautiful, bookish
Tree-lined town on the outskirts of Europe,

The air smells nimbly and sweetly of petrol
And the forest in its sunlit shroud

Of smoke and ideology reveals
That here among the Cherry Hills there lies

More history than any place can be
Imagined to accommodate, and so it burns.

Matter-of-fact as a date on a tomb,
Rebuilt from EU funds, the castle squats

On granite haunches by the slow Vrbas,
A place to keep the violence dry for now

While the chisels ring out where a single mosque
Of sixteen dynamited last time round

Is rising from its rubble to secure
A distant century against the infidel.

Smoke rises where the leaves are gathered.
More are falling. Let this warm November

Never end, and leave our group of skeletons
Companionably seated on the terrace

Beneath the black hoods of the folded umbrellas,
While the river below us flows on through itself

And away through the willows and out of sight
And we are still talking of poetry.

The Sunken Lane

Private Harry Reed, d. 24th December 1915

I mean to walk down the sunken lane
Where the dead are once more
Trying to assemble in the dark.

By the light of Bavarian gentians
I'll be looking for the dugout
At the entrance to the mine

And then descend the deepest shaft
Where the ancient ordnance
Sweats and waits implacably

For Zero Hour beneath the ridge.
I will surface in the middle of the wood
While the teams of machine-gunners

Sleep with their heads on the barrels
Just for a minute, a minute
Before the beginning, the end,

The balloon going up, the whistles
Like a cloud of nightingales.
I carry a letter from home,

The cigarette case that will save me,
A picture of you, all the time in the world
To stroke your face, while you are waiting,

Robinette or English Rose, so patiently
There at the edge of the village
Where wildflowers grow by the road.

Link-Boy

I have spent my life here, sir,
In the long nineteenth century,
Making my way as I must.

Tall as masts, the curlicued railings
Surround the great tomb, the night-magnet
For thin-shanked grave-robbers.

Rain gives consumption and syphilis
Back to the soil, where the saddle-nosed
Gravediggers bend to their labour

Then climb into the flooded pits
To re-inter themselves alive.
Here even the toadstools that burst

Like bubos from the earth are ironclad.
Defended with gallows and gunpowder
England's necropolis conquers the ocean

And drains it: the world is this island
Concealed in the fog of a triumph.
All bow at the name of Great Death.

At noon, sir, in this pitch-black street
I am your faithful link-boy
With my dark flame raised before me

A farthing, sir, yes, to extinguish.

Storm Beach

It feels like an achievement, emptiness
Reorganized to make the matter plain.
In the long pool trapped behind the shingle bank

The sky is blue and bitter. Amstel crates
And ragged scalps of weed have likewise
Been reconsidered, while the sea

Has gone somewhere as if for good:
No distance has been spared
And the horizon is revealed as yet another

Obsolescent form of measurement,
Leaving only the sublime
By which to take a sunblind bearing.

It's freezing when we stroll onstage –
We find the rake is steeper now –
As if at last we ought to broach

The fundamentals wisely put aside
Long since in weatherproof compartments
For such a day as this. But instantly it's clear

That ours will not be speaking parts.
The gulls will do all that. In this austerity
Of blazing salt-charged air and stunned geology

We're only here to represent the crowd
Who cross and go to do the greeting
And the mourning, further on and further out.

The Calm

At the mouth of the river,
Moon, stars, an Arctic calm,
The twin lights at the end of the piers
Revolving with the smoothness
We expect of supernatural machinery.

Seen from down here on the beach
The harboured ocean slowly tilts,
Like a mirror discreetly manhandled
By night from the giant room
It was supposed to occupy for ever.

The mind says *now*, but the stars
On their angelic gimbals roll
And fade, a tide of constellations
Breaking nowhere, every night
About this time. Strike up the band.

In the tumbledown bar, the singer
Has fallen from stardom and grace,
But though her interests nowadays
Are wholly secular, she can
Still refer back to the angels,

And knowing that song, we share
A moment with the saved before
We leave to make the crossing.
No captain, no ferry, but
Cross we shall, believe you me.

Melancholia

It cannot be advised. It is enforced. It leads you
Further in, armed only with this heavy iron key
That seems to sweat a coldness in your hand.

Somewhere a door awaits, a cupboard, and a book
That makes the hours redeemable. With luck. Or not.
The clocks are sleeping in the cities you have left behind

And running backwards in the ones that lie ahead
On this involuntary pilgrimage. For now, though,
Birchwood, mazy marsh, great rivers roaring to themselves

About the next bend and the next. One day you reach
A devastated plain where armoured skeletons
Lie pinned like insects to their destiny

And dogs still pick for scraps. A burnt-out waggon
Holds the still-warm ashes of an ancient library
The wind has been discarding all around,

And the corpse of its custodian, whose face resembles yours.

ii

The exhaustion of late morning! For then the mind itself
Seems to have drained its sump and left the grey of accidie
To keep you company among the freezing, shuttered streets

While men are mustered in the squares to march away,
Their soldiers' songs borne off by gales above the chimneytops,
With voivode, margrave, duke and king obliged to history

As history in turn is in their debt while it consumes them.
The women seated in the kitchen round a candle, waiting:
Shall it be embourgeoisement or death this time? The work

That frames their guarded faces cannot care, nor for the children
Sleeping in another room while plague bestirs itself
To go about the streets among the mourners, and the cannons

Speak the truth, that this is war, to breach the city walls
Behind which hides whoever is to blame or else is simply there
To pay the price in blood so that there can be peace.

Tie the key to a stone the size of your head. Let it fall
Into the well. The far-down splash means there is no forgetting.
It cannot be advised. It is enforced. But you knew that.

iii

It cannot be advised. It is enforced. At last it leads you
To the altar in the chapel of a gang of murderers
Made knights to bring God's pain to those who worship fire,

And then, since waste is sinful, strip the amber from the shore.
To pray at this stage would be vanity, you think.
It does not matter what you think: your inner emigration

Will not dignify by distance, will not hand a sentence down,
Will not at length become a special case, admired with relief
By your successors in the hitherto exhausted sphere of melancholia:

The burden of their vanity will be sufficient to ensure
That they like you can only see themselves reflected everywhere.
It cannot be advised. It is enforced. It is the sum of things.

A Closed Book

Sitting at dawn in the empty square with an émigré paper,
Sitting there reading when a cart rolled by
Piled high with bodies and the square never flinched
But went on being its stony self; sitting
While the cafes opened and the police appeared
And then took their suspicions elsewhere;
Sitting while a woman high up at a tenement window
Sang as she winched the washing out along a line
That even Blondin might have paused to think about;
Sitting and calling for breakfast as the cavalry
Rode by and broke step where the bridge begins,
So the hooves made the same sound as dogs at their bowls
Or the sudden drenching rain that was not due
Until October, when you would be here still
Doing your duty and reading the paper and watching
As if this one venue would give you
The secret entire from pogrom to bicycle,
Austerlitz to bombe surprise, the Masurian lakes,
The plague, sealed trains, the yawning sanatoria,
All of it, counterpoint, Liechtenstein, Leverkuhn's syphilis,
Girondins and Teutoburg, the works –
The daily labours of the sun and moon, the headstones
Tilting perfectly, the picturesque, the brutal, the banal – for this
Is what you spent your life preparing to absorb
As if this world, this Europe where you sat,
Existed for your planned transfiguration of the whole
Into perfection – let the others toil with doubt – for you had seen
The matter plain, and simply waited to begin.